My inventor's profile

Name: ____________________

Class: __________ Birthday: __________

Place of birth: ____________________

Two interesting facts about me:

1. ____________________

2. ____________________

Three things I'd like to invent:

1. ____________________

2. ____________________

3. ____________________

My progress passport

Inventors and innovators come from all over the world! Some of the most important inventions came from Africa and Asia (such as pottery, the wheel, glass and paper), but they were so long ago that we don't know the names of the individual inventors. This is equally true of the First Nations Australians who invented many items and continue to develop practices that show both resourcefulness and a great knowledge of science.

A

J

R

I

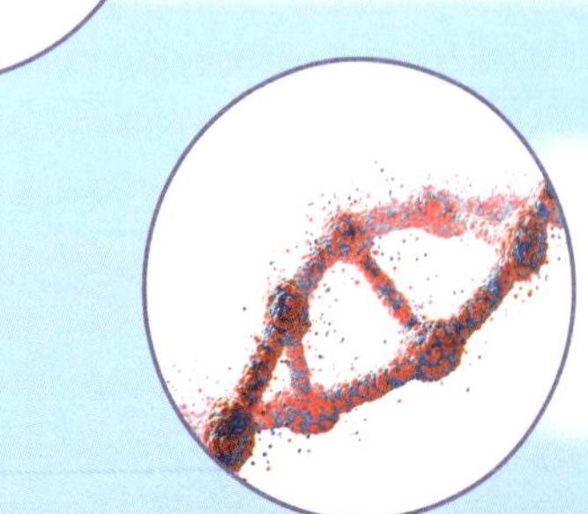

R

L
M
N
G
F
FLIGHT RECORDER DO NOT OPEN
D
J
I am ready to go on the cursive journey with you!

Before you begin writing …

Here are the **3Ps** that will help you with your writing: **p**osture, **p**encil/pen grip and **p**aper position. You will be reminded about these as you work through the book.

Posture

Relax your arms and make sure the chair supports your back. Check that your feet are flat on the floor.

Pencil/pen grip

How you hold your pencil/pen is most important. Hold your pencil/pen firmly between your thumb and index finger, balanced on your middle finger (2.5 cm before the end and not too tightly!).

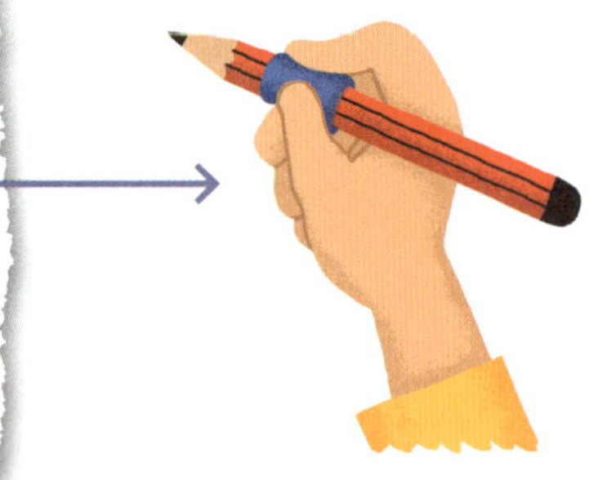

Left-handed

Right-handed

Tip! Left-handers may form some letters differently. For example, for the capital letters A, E, F, H, T, the left-handed person might go from right to left to make the join:

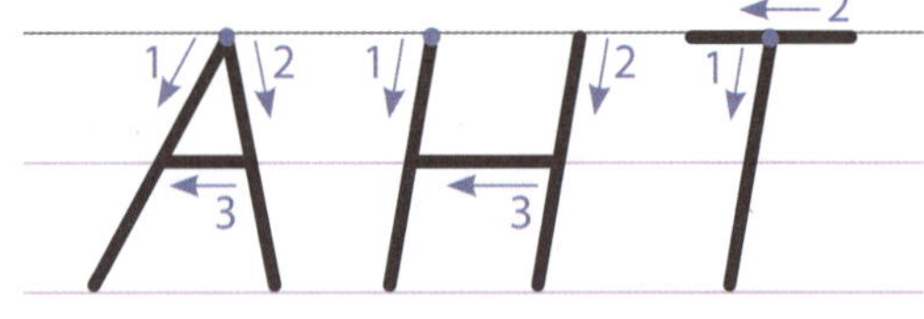

Paper position

Angle your page and use your non-writing hand to steady the page.

Left-handed

Right-handed

Revision

Queensland Beginner's print

Learning intention:

To revise Queensland Beginner's print handwriting

Before we begin on our adventure to meet all the famous inventors around the world, let's revise our print handwriting.

Trace these letters, punctuation marks and numbers.

aA bB cC dD eE fF gG

hH iI jJ kK lL mM nN

oO pP qQ rR sS tT uU

vV wW xX yY zZ

0 1 2 3 4 5 6 7 8 9 10

Copy the names of these countries. Link the capital letter to the matching lower-case letter or letters in that word, for example, Australia.

Australia Albania Barbados Georgia

Eritrea India Timor-Leste Uruguay

Exits and entries

Learning intention:
To revise letters that contain exit and entry flicks

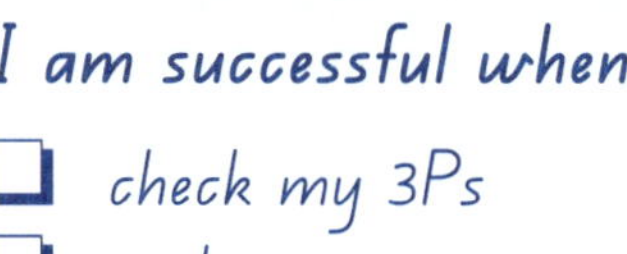

I am successful when I can:
- ❑ check my 3Ps
- ❑ make my entry and exit flicks smooth.

Trace the alphabet with all its entries and exits.

a b c d e f g h i j k l m

n o p q r s t u v w x y z

Copy the text below.

Throughout my book I will be practising my cursive handwriting, using many entries, exits and joins. I am going to try my best to make my writing fluent and easy to read. I will remember my 3Ps so that I don't become tired when I am writing a lot.

Self-assessment

- Draw a star on top of your neatest three exit flicks.
- Draw a heart on top of your neatest three entry flicks.

Fluency patterns

Learning intention: To practise my fluency joins

Take your time here to practise your fluency joins. Getting this right will help you throughout your cursive handwriting journey.

Copy these fluency patterns.

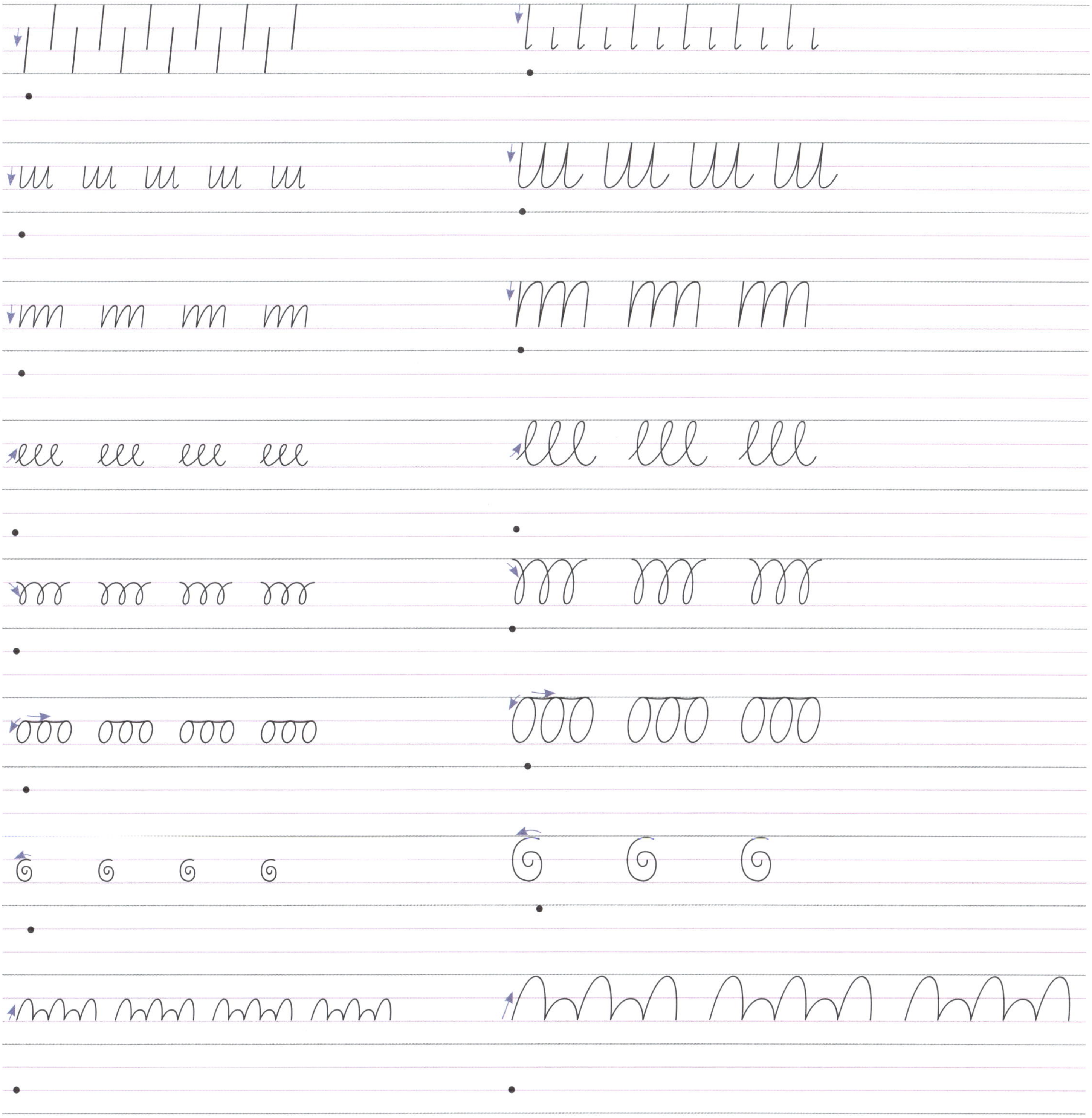

Diagonal joins

Learning intention:
To revise letters with a diagonal join

Tip!

We know a diagonal join goes from one letter's exit flick up to meet the next letter. Practise the diagonal joins below. Remember, the pencil/pen stays on the paper.

Trace and then copy these diagonal joins.

ai am an ap ar au ay

ce cu cy de di du dy

en em ei ey he hi hu

Copy this sentence to practise your diagonal joins.

Creativity and effort shape the world.

You can write more quickly and easily if you write in cursive.

Diagonal joins to tall letters

Learning intention:
To use diagonal joins with tall letters

Trace and then copy these diagonal joins.

Copy this sentence to practise your diagonal joins.

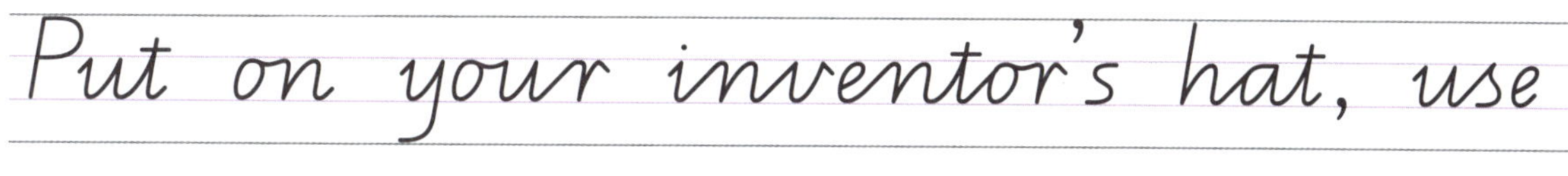

your imagination and make history!

Drop-in joins

Learning intention:
To write letters that are dropped into place with a drop-in join

When we join to anti-clockwise letters (such as a, c, d, g and q), the exit from the first letter reaches high towards the top of the anti-clockwise letter. Take the exit flick up high!
Then lift your pencil, and drop in the anti-clockwise letter to join with the exit flick.

The a touches the exit here.

Trace and then copy these drop-in joins for a, c, d, g and q.

la ia ha ac ec uc ed id ld

ag ma ig aq eq ng ca ud nq

Trace and then copy these words, which include letters with drop-in joins.

Alexander Graham Bell invented the

telephone in 1876. Two cans linked by

a string will show you how.

Horizontal joins

Learning intention:
To write letters with horizontal joins

Tip! The horizontal join from f is angled so it's easier to join to the next letter. The horizontal join for o, r, v and w has a slight dip. Don't lift your pencil when making horizontal joins to clockwise letters.

slight dip

fi on ri vu wi

Trace and then copy these horizontal joins.

oi om on op or ou ov

ri rm rn rp rr ru rv

vi vu vv vy vi vu vv

wi wm wn wr wy wi

fi fn fy ra vo wa ri

vm rm oy ry vy wy wn

Horizontal joins to anti-clockwise letters

Learning intention:

To write anti-clockwise letters with horizontal joins

When writing horizontal joins to anti-clockwise letters, go across to the start of the letter, then **retrace**.

oa

Trace and then copy these letter pairs and words.

[illegible] oc oo og os od oa oc oo

[illegible] rc ro rg rs rd ri oi vi

[illegible] wc wo fa fo fc va vo

[illegible] aeroplane vibrations radio

[illegible] phonograph waves forward

[illegible] focus extra arrival order

[illegible] goaded graceful dose roll

Horizontal joins to tall letters

Learning intention:

To join short letters to tall letters

I am successful when I can:

- ❑ check my 3Ps
- ❑ write horizontal joins to tall letters.

When you make a join to tall letters, go right to the top and then retrace a little as you move downwards.

ok

Trace and then copy these letter pairs.

ol ob ok ol ok of

rl rk rt rb rh rt

vk vl vt vt vb vf

rf wl wt ot wb rb

Self-assessment

Assess your horizontal joins.

❑ I need some more practice

❑ I'm making progress

❑ I've got it!

Teacher comment

Letters that do not join

Learning intention:
To write letters that have clockwise finishers

Letters that finish in a clockwise direction do not join.

b g j p s y z

Trace and then copy these letters that finish in a clockwise direction.

b g j p s y

Copy these letter pairs and words on the lines below.

ba baby be bean ga gave

go goal ji jigsaw jo joke

pa paper po pot sa sails

si sight ye yes yo young

za zap zo zoo zo zoom

The letter q does not join

The letter q finishes in an anticlockwise direction, but it also does not join.

qu

Learning intention:
To practise writing the letter q

Trace and then copy these letter pairs with qu.

qu qu qu qu qu qu

Copy these words and then draw a line to match each word to its picture. The first one is done for you.

queen quilt quiet quick quokka

queen

Capital letters

Remember that capital letters do not join.

Learning intention:
To write words with capital letters

Trace and then copy these capital letters on the lines below.

A B C D E F G

H I J K L M N

O P Q R S T U

V W X Y Z

Copy these place names.

Brisbane Queensland Australia

The Whitsundays Gold Coast

Lawn Hill Gorge Cape Tribulation

Copy the sentence below, which includes letters that do and do not join.

James Chadwick was an English physicist. He discovered neutrons, for which he received the Nobel Prize in Physics in 1935. One of the Moon's craters is named after him.

Self-assessment Assess how you are going with letters that do not join.

- ❑ I need some more practice

- ❑ I'm making progress

- ❑ I've got it!

Teacher comment

Consolidating

Learning intention:

To review my print handwriting

Remember to always use printing for the labels on maps and diagrams.

Label the diagram with the words at the bottom of the page. Use print handwriting. One is done for you.

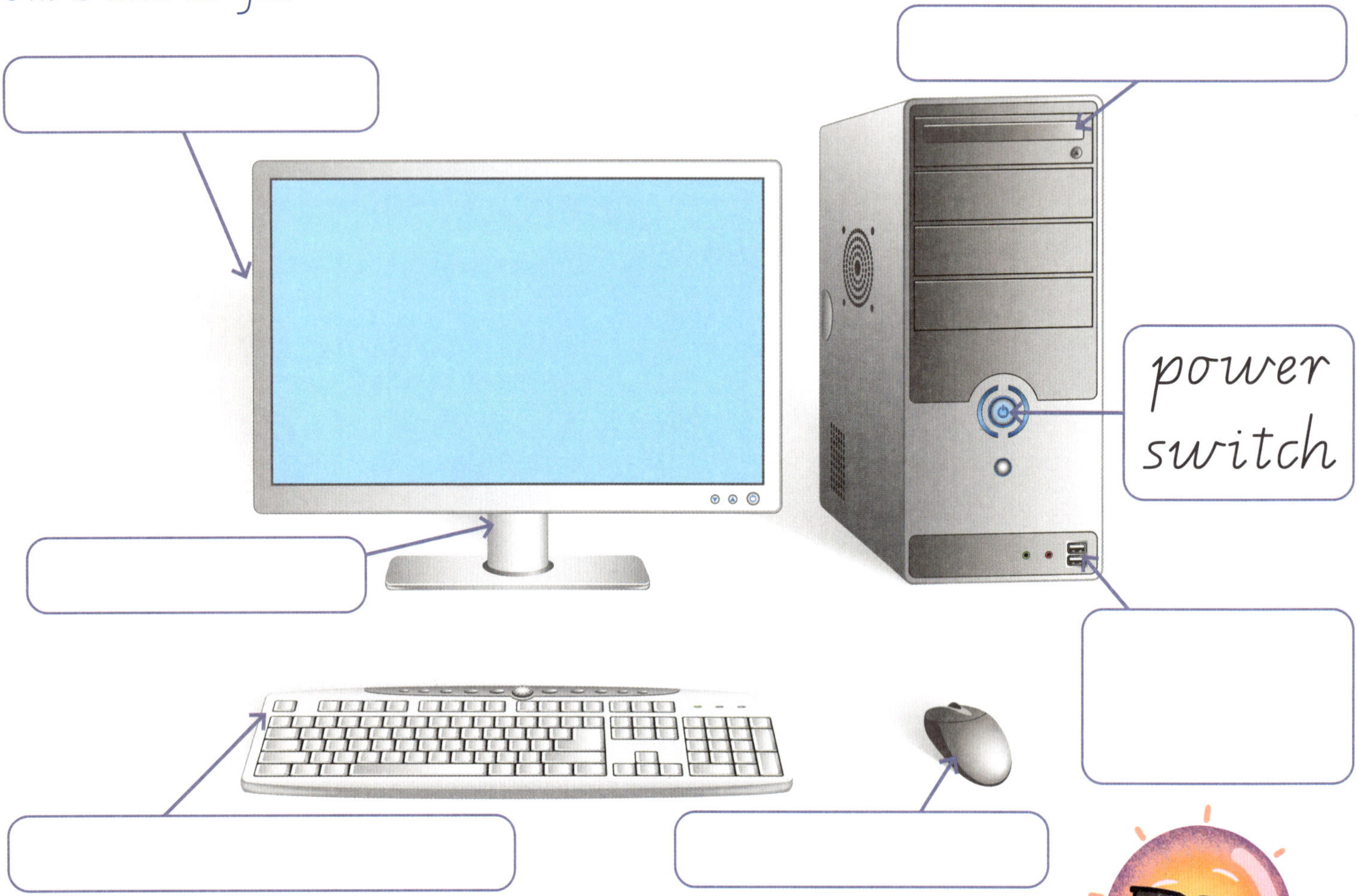

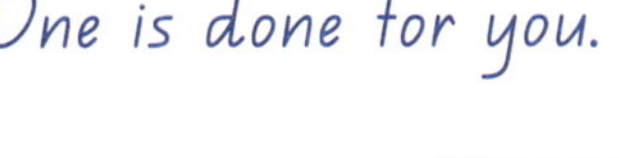

power switch

This older computer looks different from a laptop or tablet, but you can see how they have some of the same features.

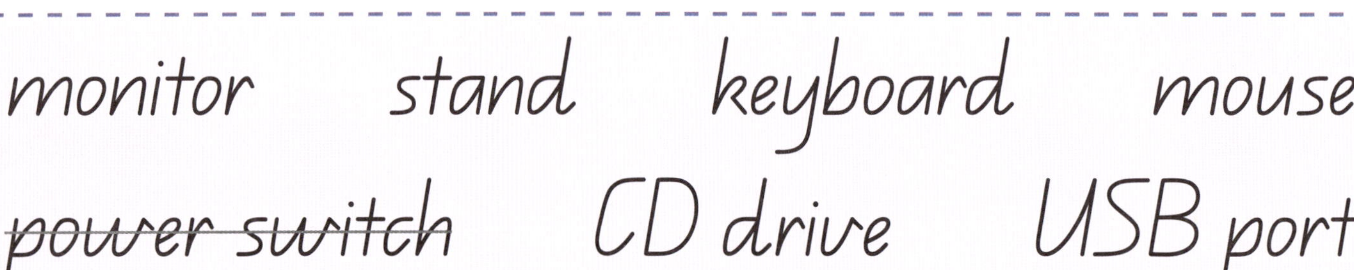

Assessment: All joins

With three different coloured pencils or highlighters, shade the letter pairs to identify the different joins in this box.

Colour the diagonal joins in one colour. Then colour the horizontal joins in a different colour. Lastly, colour the drop-in joins in another colour. Not all of these letters do join, so some squares will be left uncoloured.

I am successful when I can:

- ❑ check my 3Ps
- ❑ write letters that contain joins.

mp	Fa	al	xy	fi
ac	If	Lm	ox	of
be	ng	cr	Ja	oh
hi	or	de	po	rk

Self-assessment

Assess how you are going with all joins.

❑ I need some more practice

❑ I'm making progress

❑ I've got it!

Teacher comment

Practising joins

Joins to s

Learning intention:
To join our letters to the letter s

Tip! When we do horizontal joins to connect letters to s, it requires some retracing at the top of the finishing letters.
Go across to form the top of the s, then retrace the top on your way down.

Trace these horizontal joins to s. Then copy these joins in the space beside the letters.

rs vs ws fs

rs vs ws fs

When we have words with double s, the first and second letter look the same: either both short or both like the regular s.

Trace and then copy these words.

first cross position chefs

closer verse rainbows boost

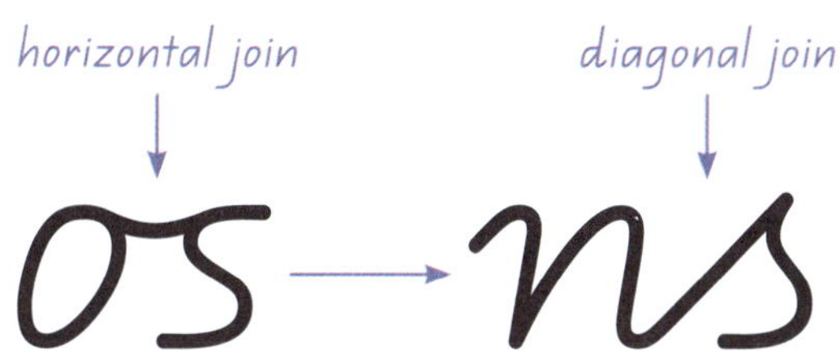

Learning intention:
To practise joins to the shorter s

When we use diagonal joins to connect letters to s, the s changes to a short s. Did you know that the shorter s will make your writing faster? Try it and see.

Trace and then copy these letter pairs to practise diagonal joins to the shorter s.

as cs ds es is ls ms ns

poems pods beams best

Trace and then copy these letter pairs and words to practise your diagonal and horizontal joins to s.

as cs ds es hs is ks ls ms ns

atoms optics myths

os rs vs ws os rs vs ws os rs

mirrors videos wheelbarrows

Trace and then copy these words.

hands best last this cakes music

sunset cracks bells fishing tracks

fashion physics invents seams myths

Trace and copy these sentences.

There are always new innovations in technology. What is something completely new that you would love to see in your lifetime? Would it be to teleport to a new place, or even to another time? You could time travel to the past and ride on a penny-farthing bike.

Joins to e

Learning intention: To write a horizontal join to e

smooth diagonal join

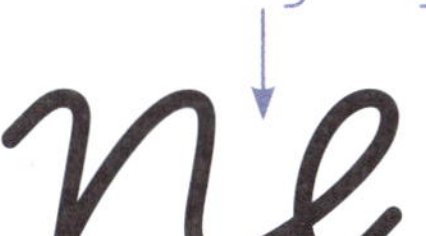

Diagonal joins to e are a smooth upward stroke. We don't connect horizontal joins to the letter e. So o, r, v and w do not join up to e.

no horizontal join to e

oe re ve we

Trace and then copy this pattern.

Trace and then copy these letter pairs in the space on the same line.

oe re ve we

Trace and then copy these words.

poems whichever save vessel core believe

travel before stare weather canoe

volcanoes breathe achieve alive answer

Joins to f

Learning intention:
To practise the looped f

Tip!

When writing diagonal joins to f, the f is looped at the top.

The letter f at the beginning of a word or after a pencil lift looks like this: f

When letters join to f it is written line this: f

Use a diagonal join to practise these joins to f.

af ef if uf lf af ef if uf lf

calf sniff before raffle yourself puff

life reef strife

unify whiff afloat

Did you know?
Rosalind Franklin created the first X-ray picture of DNA, called Photo 51, which helped lead to the discovery of the molecular structure of DNA.

Passport

Self-assessment Draw a star on your neatest three joins to f.

I am successful when I can:

- ❑ add a horizontal join to f.

Trace and then copy these letter pairs and words to practise horizontal joins to f.

scarf lift-off surf coffee snowfall

Trace and then copy these words with joins to and from the letter f.

lift fiftieth fishing fixed magnify

Copy this sentence.

Ms Orfanos fished

for five hours at

the surf beach.

Joins to x

Learning intention: *To join our letters to and from the letter x*

Always cross the letter x before you write the next letter.

Make a high exit from the first stroke of x, cross the x and then write the next letter.

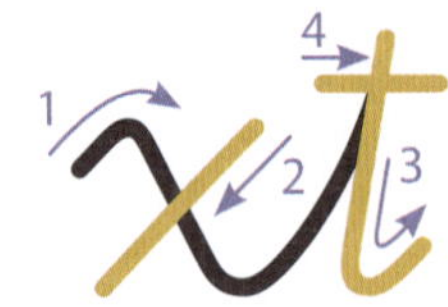

Trace and then copy these letter pairs and words to practise your joins to and from x.

excitement exploration excellence fix box

extra exercise exchange except excess

Copy this sentence using your neatest cursive writing.

The clever fox moved extremely fast. His quick reflexes helped him to avoid a trap. He fixed his eyes on escape and made it safely to his warm and cosy den.

Consolidating

Learning intention:
To review all I have learnt with cursive handwriting

Copy these sentences.

Did you know that the technology to create wireless networks was invented in Australia? In 1992, Dr John O'Sullivan and the CSIRO developed technology to reduce the echo of radio waves, which allows wifi to work. It is now used by billions of people and has changed the way we live. Do you use wifi at school?

Copy these sentences.

Cameras from years ago were heavy, bulky and awkward to handle. They were very sensitive to changes in light levels, and any shaking would make the photo look blurred. These days, cameras are small, portable and can even be used underwater.

Assessment: Practising joins

Copy this selection of inventions. With a coloured pencil, go over any drop-in, horizontal or diagonal joins.

telephone typewriter handwriting

fruit peeler battery kettle

nail sewing machine alarm clock

compass computer black box

jet ski remote control telephone

Complete the following sentence on the lines below.

My favourite invention is ____________________

because ____________________.

Self-assessment

Assess how you are going with tricky joins.

❑ I need some more practice

❑ I'm making progress

❑ I've got it!

Teacher comment

More practice with joins

Getting faster

Copy the sentences below to practise your joins.

Galileo Galilei (1564–1642), an Italian astronomer and mathematician, is known as the father of modern astronomy and physics. His improvements to the telescope led to key astronomical discoveries. Albert Einstein credited Galileo as being more responsible for the birth of modern science than any other person.

Copy these sentences.

Darri saw some flying fish flip, flop, flap and float in the air. She wondered if these fish had inspired Leonardo da Vinci to envisage a flying machine, which he did many drawings of. She resolved to look this up when she got back home.

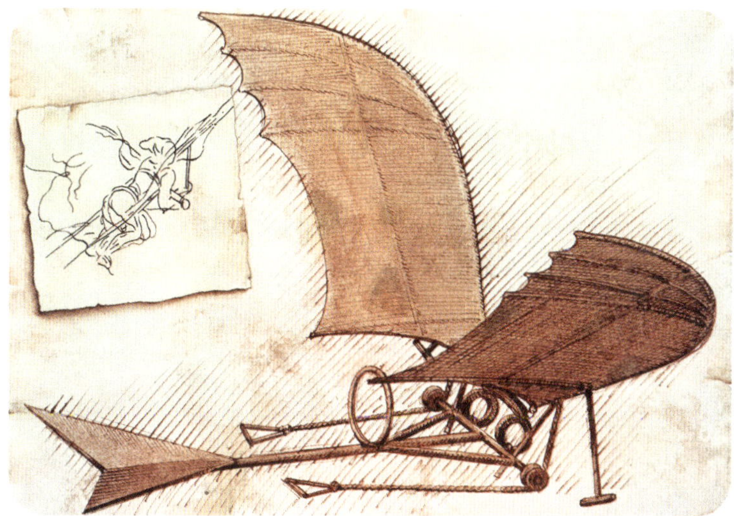

Practise writing these words.

cow snow Liv lotto grow two

window potato also buffalo Gustav

Fine motor skills task: Colour in this picture. Then add a description using words from the list above.

Double letters

Learning intention:

To practise letter pairs and words with double letters

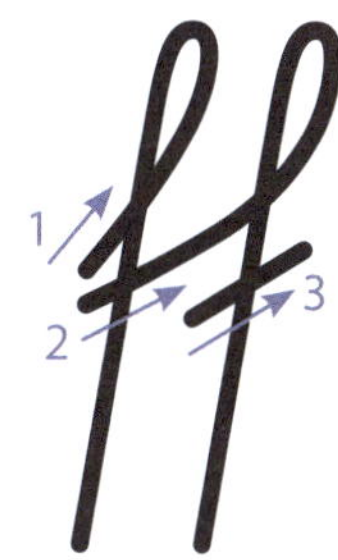

Make sure your double letters are not too far apart. Remember, when joining to f the letter is looped and the crossbar joins to the next letter. The double f follows the same rule.

Trace and then copy these letter pairs.

dd ee ff gg ll mm nn oo

pp rr tt zz cc bb cc ss

Copy these words with double letters.

address keen wiggle terrestrial app pool

cliff sunny worry bedazzle valley

broccoli fluff poppy bubble hiccup

withhold messy watt savvy bookkeeper

For better fluency, use one crossbar for double t, like this: tt

For the letter r, you can decide whether to join it to the next letter or not. Which way is quicker for you? rr rr

Practise your joins to and from double r and double t by copying these letters and words.

arr err irr urr rra rry rru att utt

flurry surrounds occurrence corrosive

pattern battery attempt clutter

When you write a double s, the letters should look the same. So diagonal joins use the shorter s, and the horizontal joins use the regular s.

miss moss

Practise your joins to and from double s and double t by copying these letters and words.

ess iss sso sse ssi oss uss ssu

massive colossal access dossier engross

attempt clutter pattern battery

Trace and then copy this text.

On 16 July 1969, NASA launched the

spacecraft Apollo 11 into space from NASA's

Kennedy Space Center. Four days later,

millions of people watched astronauts

Neil Armstrong and Edwin "Buzz" Aldrin

walk on the Moon. The third astronaut,

Michael Collins, did not land on the Moon.

However, the mission would not have been

possible without his skills as

a command module pilot.

Consolidating

Learning intention: To practise cursive handwriting

Copy the following text to practise your cursive handwriting.

Sir Isaac Newton was an English scientist and mathematician. He explained gravity and developed the theory of colour. Newton's experiments of light and colour were a great contribution to our world. His "crucial experiment" proved that light is made up of different colours, rather than light being coloured by a prism.

Self-assessment

Assess your cursive handwriting.

❑ I need some more practice

❑ I'm making progress

❑ I've got it!

Teacher comment

Assessment: More practice with joins

Copy these words with double letters.

effort accident allow boost paraffin

Copy the double r, double s and double t words below.

current hurry glass battery possess

impress letter buttonhole crossword ferry

Copy these words with double letters.

didgeridoo cello hollow arrow fluff

wiggle constellation stellar furrow valley

mission satellite wobble mass parallel

Self-assessment

Assess your joins to double letters.

❑ I need some more practice

❑ I'm making progress

❑ I've got it!

Teacher comment

Handwriting hints

Letter size and spacing

Learning intention:
To focus on the size and spacing of my letters

I am successful when I can:

- ❏ check my 3Ps
- ❏ write faster using smaller lines.

Don't let your horizontal joins go too far before connecting to the next letter.

Focus on your letter size and spacing as you copy these sentences.

Marie Curie was a Polish-French physicist

and chemist who discovered polonium

and radium, and conducted research on

radioactivity. She was the first woman to

win a Nobel prize and the first person to

win two Nobel prizes in different sciences.

When World War I broke out in Europe,

Curie realised that X-rays could help doctors

to work out what was wrong with injured

soldiers. Curie and her daughter Irène set

up 200 radiology units during the first

two years of the war, which helped to save

many lives. Her research also led to the

use of radiation to treat cancer. The legacy

of Curie's work has contributed to shaping

life in the 21st century.

Self-assessment

Assess how you are going with letter size and spacing.

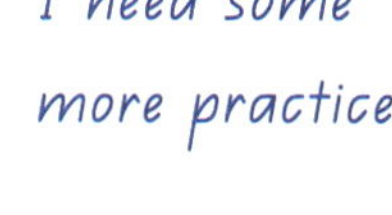

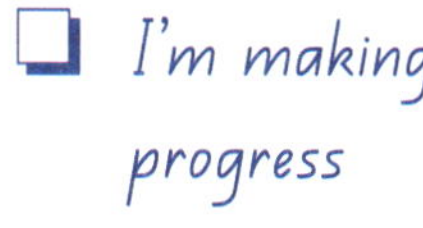

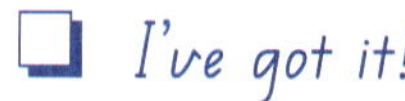

- ❏ I need some more practice
- ❏ I'm making progress
- ❏ I've got it!

Teacher comment

Spacing between letters

Learning intention:

To focus on the size and spacing between letters

I am successful when I can:

- ❑ check my 3Ps
- ❑ write faster on smaller lines.

Tip! **Kerning:** (noun) The spacing between letters in a word. All letters in words should be as evenly spaced as possible. This makes your writing neater and easier to read.

computer

Rewrite the word "computer" with even letter spacing on the lines below.

computer ✗ — uneven spacing

computer ✗ — not enough spacing

computer ✓ — correct spacing

These letter pairs do not have the correct spacing. Rewrite them with the correct spacing.

ai ld hi ck le tt ay

wh ed ry op oo nd th

Self-assessment

Assess your spacing between letters.

- ❑ I need some more practice
- ❑ I'm making progress
- ❑ I've got it!

Teacher comment

Spacing between words

Learning intention:
To focus on the spacing between words

I am successful when I can:
- ❑ check my 3Ps
- ❑ make spaces even
- ❑ write letters of the same size.

Looking at these sound waves, you can see spaces. There is also a space bar on the keyboard. We need spaces in sound, in our typing and in our writing to make sense of things.

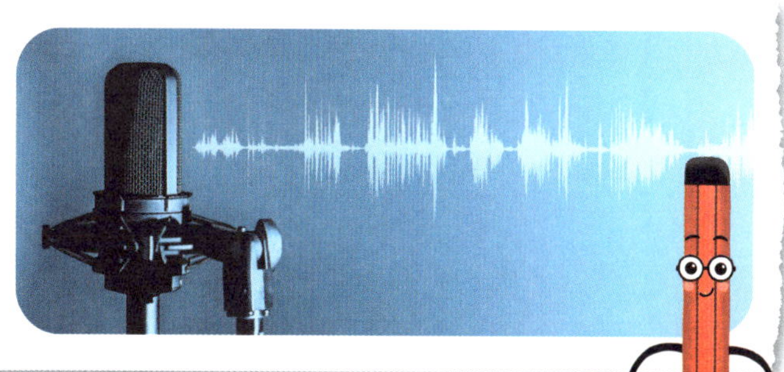

Rewrite this passage, using even spaces between the words.

When words are too close together or too far apart, it makes the writing difficult to read. The spaces between words need to be even, and letters must be of the same size. When we do this,   the writing is much easier to read.

Copy this passage, keeping a consistent size for your letters and even spaces between the words.

Professor Fiona Wood is a British-born Australian plastic surgeon and burns specialist who lives in Perth. Professor Wood and her co-inventor, Marie Stoner, invented "spray-on skin" to help people with burns. This technique was a world first and has saved the lives of thousands of people who have suffered severe burns. In 2005 Fiona Wood was named Australian of the Year.

Slope

Learning intention: To write using a slope

Having a consistent slope makes writing easier to read. Using a slight slope to the right makes it easier to control your pen, and so your writing looks neater and easier to read.

✗ Sparky

✓ Sparky

Trace and then copy these fluency patterns with the slope card.

Copy these words, keeping a consistent slope.

slope handwriting cursive angle direction

mountain crater tilt orbit eclipse

typewriter bicycle stapler lawnmower chess

Consolidating

Survey ten people in your class. Ask them which one of these inventions they would not want to give up. Use tally marks to collect your data.

Computer	Washing machine	Electric toothbrush	Video-game console

Present your information in a column graph below. Remember to label your graph.

In cursive handwriting, write two comments about the information you have gathered, such as the most or least popular invention.

1.

2.

Copy these sentences, focusing on the spacing, size and slope.

Rachel Carson was an American marine biologist and conservationist. In 1962 she wrote an influential book called "Silent Spring", which exposed the harmful effects of pesticides on the environment. Credited with advancing the global environmental movement, she once said, "One way to open your eyes is to ask yourself, 'What if I had never seen this before?'"

Assessment: Handwriting hints

Rewrite the following sentences in cursive handwriting, using the correct spacing, size and slope.

I am successful when I can:

- ❑ write my words with even spaces
- ❑ write letters with a slope
- ❑ write letters with a consistent size.

Do you ever daydream about building or inventing something? How would you get started? Would you create winner wheels, memory machines or awesome aircraft? Wilbur and Orville Wright (the Wright Brothers) were among the first to build and fly an aeroplane with an engine.

Self-assessment

Assess how you are going with spacing, size and slope.

❑ I need some more practice

❑ I'm making progress

❑ I've got it!

Teacher comment

Letters and words

Learning intention: *To practise our fluency*

Copy the letters and sentences below to practise your fluency.

abcdefghijklmnopqrstuvwxyz

Peter practised golf every day for weeks.

He took golf lessons and practised his putting, chipping and driving to improve his golf and lower his handicap score.

What a great sport!

Common blends and digraphs

Learning intention:
To practise common blends and digraphs

Trace these common blends (letter combinations in which each letter makes a sound) and words. Copy them on the lines below and then add two more words of your own for each letter combination.

gr great green

pl plan please

nd bland grand

bl blue black

nk blank thank

spr spring sprung

squ squash squid

tr tree trunk

ch chick chatter

ft soft left

br bridge break

lt belt felt

thr three through

scr scrape screen

br brother brainwave

dr drink drum

gl glamour gloomy

Trace and then copy these digraphs (two letters that make one sound) and words. Remember to use the correct joins. Then add two more words of your own for each digraph.

oa throat float

ea leaf deaf

ch reach beach

th throw think

gh laugh cough

sh ship sharp

oo pool didgeridoo

ee sheep need

ie chief brief

ei receive ceiling

Rewrite these words, including the prefix. For example, un- + happy = unhappy. The first one is done for you.

un- happy tidy do likely

dis- appear like able trust

re- arrange appear write

tri- angle cycle athlete pod

mis- place use understand

First Nations Australians cut bark from trees, without damaging the trees, to create watertight canoes (above). They also made the didgeridoo (right), a wind instrument, from hollowed-out trees or branches.

Practise cursive writing

Copy the two words on each line and then use both words in a short sentence on the line below. The first one is done for you.

Remember that your sentences need to make sense. Try saying them out loud to check.

friends friends because because

I like my friends because we have fun.

next school

girl stopped

queen window

fish jumped

animals sun

floppy tree

green garden

everyone shouted

another way

dark suddenly

better town

think king

wish different

keep key

water fun

everyone asked

Self-assessment Circle your three neatest words in cursive handwriting.

Revision

Learning intention: To revise cursive handwriting

Copy the text below to practise your spacing, size and slope.

Nikola Tesla was a Serbian-American scientist and inventor who specialised in working with electricity. He took after his mother, who was a scientist and had an enormous passion for science. Tesla worked with Thomas Edison until they had a major disagreement on the type of electricity to use for new inventions. This led Tesla to found his own company, the Tesla Electric Light Company.

Copy these sentences.

Australian David Warren invented the black box flight recorder in 1954. These recorders (which are actually orange) let air-crash investigators listen to conversations and retrieve flight data recorded before the crash. This helps to work out the cause of a crash. In 1967, Australia became the first country to make the black box mandatory in major aircraft.

Consolidating

Learning intention: To present our work neatly

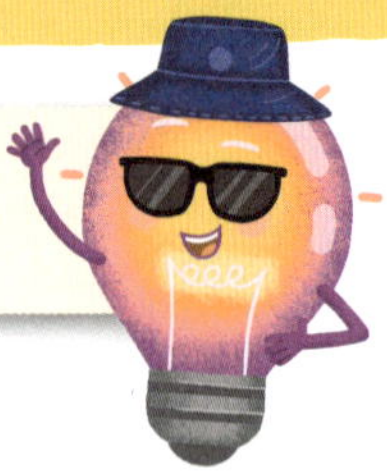

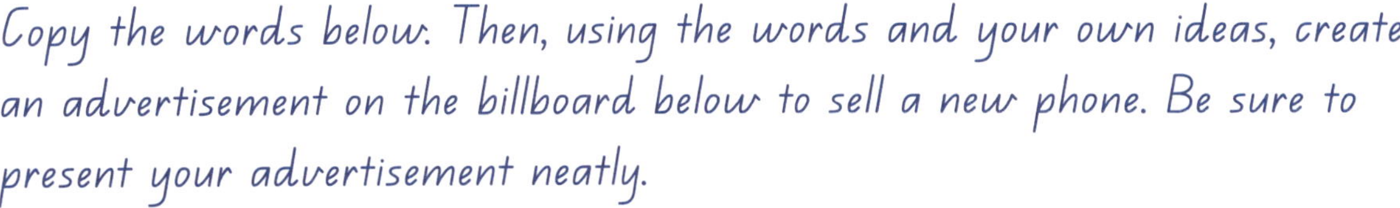

Copy the words below. Then, using the words and your own ideas, create an advertisement on the billboard below to sell a new phone. Be sure to present your advertisement neatly.

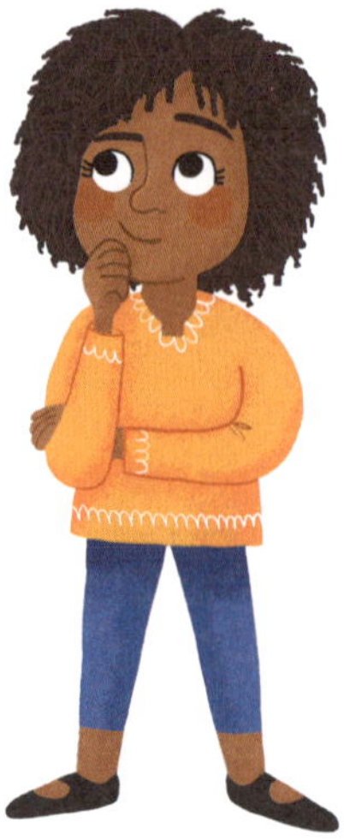

sale best price music volume

apps technology photos charger

invention camera features warranty

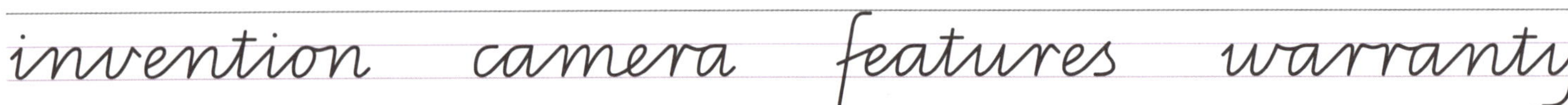

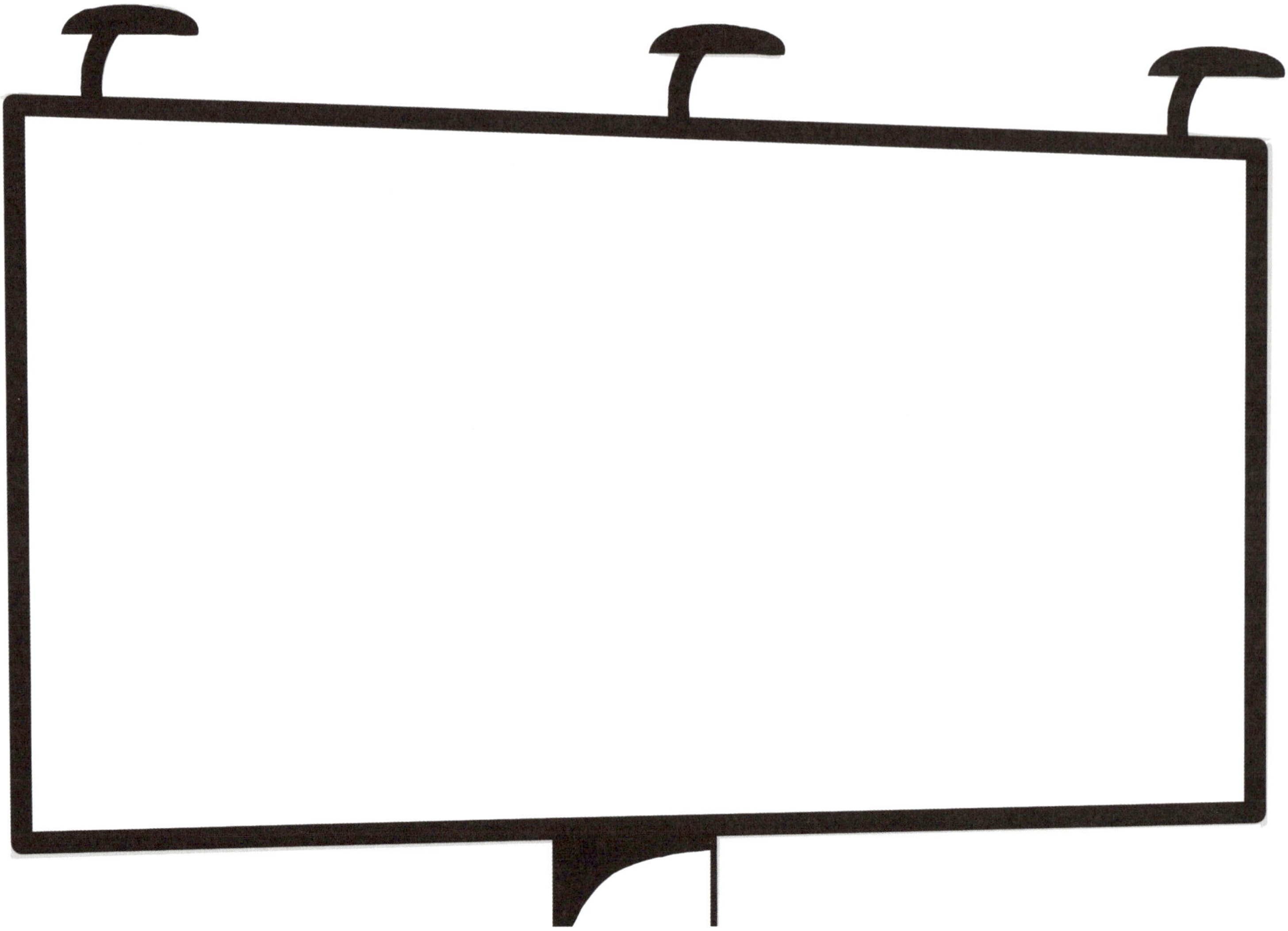

Assessment: Fluency and legibility

Rewrite these sentences in cursive handwriting. Assess your handwriting at the bottom of the page.

In this book, you have become familiar with different inventors from various countries: the United Kingdom, Poland, Italy, France, Serbia, the United States of America and Australia. They have all had a major influence on our world.

Test your memory. On a separate piece of paper, list as many of the inventors you've read about in this book as you can. Then check to see if you've missed any. Remember to go back and fill in your passport.

Self-assessment

Assess the fluency and legibility of your handwriting.

❑ I need some more practice

❑ I'm making progress

❑ I've got it!

Teacher comment

Consolidation

Punctuation marks

Learning intention:
To write and revise punctuation marks

Edit the text below by filling in the missing letters and the correct punctuation. The words in bold are defined in the glossary that follows the text.

Louis Pasteur was born on 20 December 1822
_e was born in Dole, France _asteur
was skilled in drawing and painting
gaining a Bachelor of Arts degree in 1840
_his talented man was also interested
in science and later gained a Bachelor
of Science degree _asteur was one of the
most famous **microbiologists** in history
_id you know that his findings changed
the world of medicine forever _asteur
studied researched and then invented a
whole new process where bacteria could be
removed by boiling water _his became
known as **pasteurisation** _n 1879 _asteur
invented the first vaccine _hrough

_asteur's discovery of **vaccines** thousands of people have survived fatal illnesses _n incredible innovator microbiologist artist and scientist _ouis _asteur died on 28 September 1895 at the age of 72 _asteur once said, Science knows no country, because knowledge belongs to humanity. _is legacy changed the world

Glossary

microbiologist: an expert in microorganisms

pasteurisation: sterilisation of a product to make it safe to consume

vaccine: a substance used to produce antibodies to fight disease

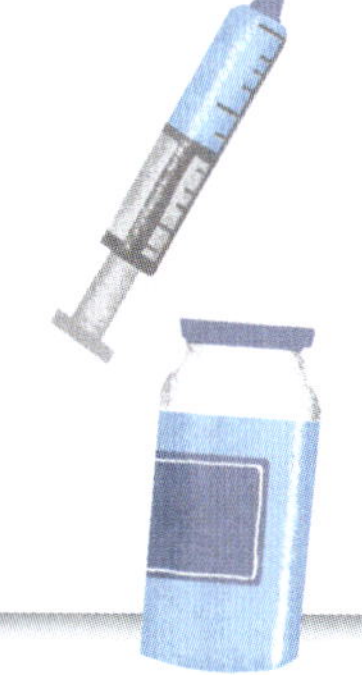

I am successful when I have included:

- ❑ 16 capital letters
- ❑ 10 full stops
- ❑ 8 commas
- ❑ 1 question mark
- ❑ 1 set of speech marks
- ❑ 1 exclamation mark.

Self-assessment

Assess your punctuation marks.

❑ I need some more practice

❑ I'm making progress

❑ I've got it!

Teacher comment

Numerals

Copy these number words and then write them as numerals. The first one is done for you.

ninety-two

ninety-two 92

twelve

eighty-five

fourteen

fifty-eight

five hundred

two thousand

seventy-three

Write these numerals as words.

99

14

296

408

840

1500

OXFORD UNIVERSITY PRESS

Complete these number patterns.

5 10 15 20 __ __ __ __

2 5 8 11 __ __ __ __

3 5 7 9 __ __ __ __ __

16 14 12 __ __ __ __

22 33 44 55 66 77 __ __

4 8 12 16 __ __ __ __

100 150 200 250 ____ ____ ____

90 85 80 75 __ __ __ __

Complete the fact file about a famous inventor in this book, or you can write about another inventor that you know.

Inventor's name:

Date of birth: ___ / ___ / _____

Country of birth:

Invention or discovery:

Description of invention or discovery:

Timeline

You will know the answers from reading this book. (You can see the page reference in brackets at the end of each information box.)

Match the invention to the correct year on the timeline, and then complete the answer on the line provided.

The CSIRO and __________ developed technology to reduce the echo of radio waves, which allowed wifi to work. (See page 27.)

Write the name of one of the astronauts on Apollo 11, which made the first crewed landing on the Moon. (See page 35.)

This invention is used to help find out what happened when a plane crashes. (See page 55.)

This Australian of the Year specialises in burns treatments. (See page 42.)

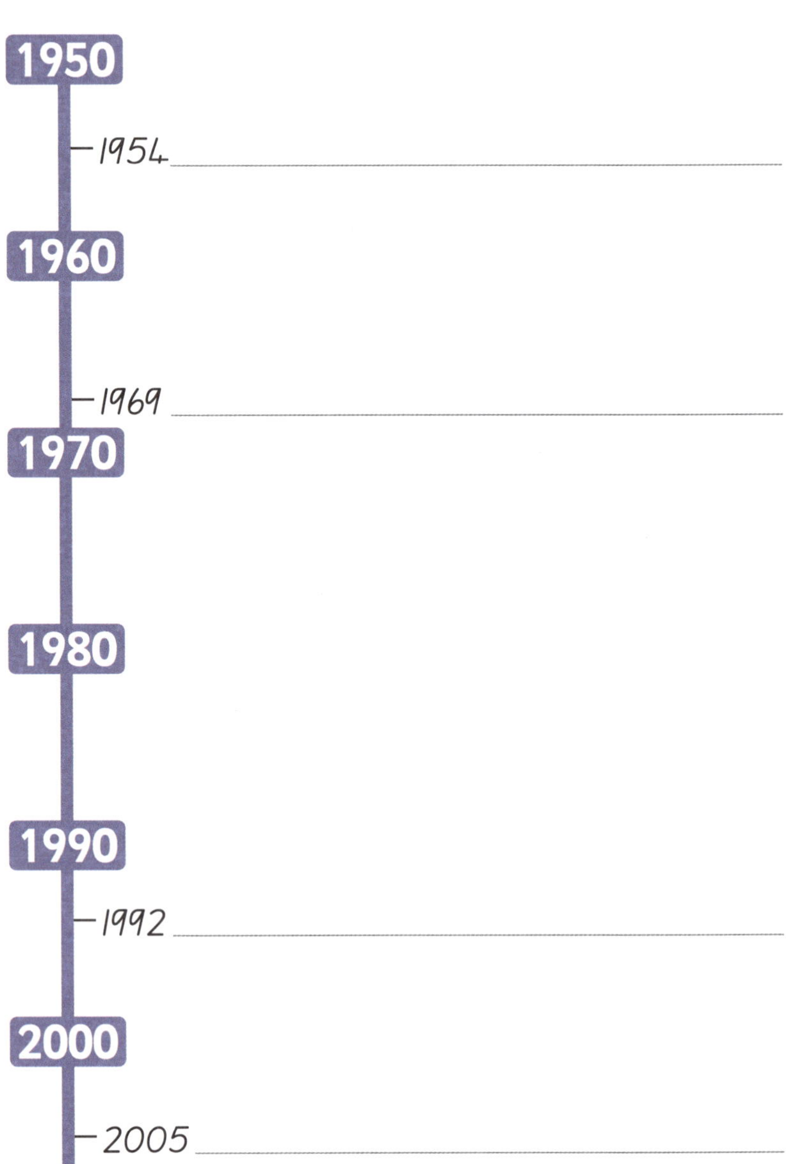

Crossword

The number in brackets following the clue is the number of letters in each word. Your teacher can see the completed crossword in the Teacher Resources on Oxford Owl. There are extra clues there as well. Try to write neatly in the middle of each square and use capital letters.

Across

3. The name for what we do when we write letters on an angle (5 letters)
5. Marie Curie conducted research on this (13 letters)
8. Something that separates words (5 letters)
9. A good _____ is important when holding a pencil (4 letters)
10. Birth country of Louis Pasteur (6 letters)

Down

1. Someone who creates inventions (8 letters)
2. Throughout this book I have learnt _________ handwriting (7 letters)
4. Used to take photos (6 letters)
6. Alexander Graham Bell's invention (9 letters)
7. It is important to go back over or ______ when doing horizontal joins to anti-clockwise letters. (7 letters)

Independent writing

Write about any of the inventors or inventions that you know of or have learnt about below. Remember to use your best cursive handwriting.